D1708396

Table of Contents

Eagles in America

Bald eagles are essential to the United States's sense of history and pride. Native Americans believed bald eagles to be messengers between their people and the gods. Many Native Americans still use bald eagle feathers in their headdresses and ceremonies.

Native American headdress

In 1782, the U.S. Congress adopted the bald eagle as a symbol of the new nation. Since then, the bald eagle has been displayed on the Great Seal of the United States and is imprinted on U.S. currency. If you have a quarter, take a look at the back of it. The eagle represented there is a bald eagle.

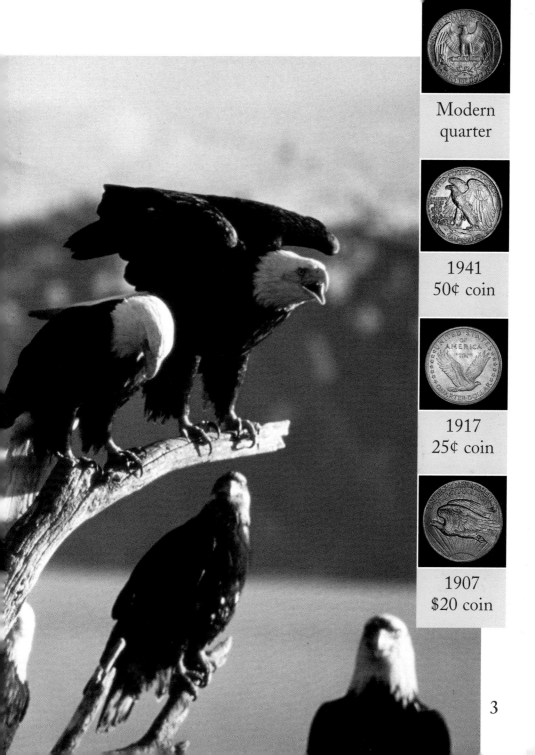

Modern
quarter

1941
50¢ coin

1917
25¢ coin

1907
$20 coin

3

Bald eagles live in many different places throughout the United States and Canada. The largest U.S. gathering is in Alaska, but large populations also live in Florida, along the East Coast and West Coast, and in the Upper Midwest. Today, there are more than 4,000 nesting pairs of bald eagles in the United States, but that has not always been the case. Earlier in the century, bald eagles were in danger of *extinction*.

A Keen-Eyed Raptor

Bald eagles are among the largest *raptors* in North America. They range from thirty to forty inches tall. The birds have a *wingspan* of seven to eight feet, and weigh from eight to fourteen pounds. The females are larger than the males. The eagles' heads are white, giving

them the appearance of baldness. "Balde" is an old English word for white. When Europeans first populated America, they may very well have referred to bald eagles as white eagles.

A bald eagle's wingspan can be seven to eight feet.

A bald eagle can see things up to eight times better than humans can. A bald eagle can spot a mouse or rabbit or fish from hundreds of feet away. Bald eagles have large *talons*, which they use to capture their *prey*. Their curved *beaks* help them tear into their food. They often dive out of the sky to capture a fish or mammal, then carry it away to eat it. Bald eagles also eat *carrion* – animals and fish that are already dead.

A bald eagle swoops down,
skims the water's surface, and catches a fish.

Bald eagle talons

Bald eagles migrate each year along *flyways*, which are routes that the birds navigate annually to reach their summer or winter homes. In spring, the eagles fly north, and in autumn, they fly south, wintering along the river valleys and coasts of Canada and the United States. The eagles congregate in places where game and fish are plentiful, such as in pine forests that border rivers. The birds particularly like to gather near dams where salmon and other fish *spawn*. These fish provide the eagles with an ample food supply.

10

Leaving the Nest

Bald eagles mate for life. When a male and female eagle first meet, they engage in an elaborate *courtship display* in which they lock their talons and cartwheel through the sky. They build their nests, called *aeries,* high up in pine trees to protect their young from predators. Bald eagles will use

Young bald eagle in nest

the same nest year after year, adding material each year they return. A nest, which is made out of sticks and leaves, may be three feet wide and three feet deep when the eagles first build it. But after many years, it can become much larger. Nests that measure more than

eight feet wide and ten feet deep have been reported.

Courtship display

13

A bald eagle usually lays one or two eggs each spring. The parents take turns *brooding* the eggs until they hatch, which usually takes thirty-five to forty days. While one parent watches over the nest, the other hunts for food and protects the

Bald eagle eggs

territory around the nest. Some bald eagles defend a territory of twenty square miles.

14

When the *eaglets* hatch, they are covered with gray *down*, which is replaced by dark brown feathers within a few weeks. The adults feed the eaglets for several months. When the eaglets are three months old, they begin to fly. After the eaglets learn to fly, the adults supply less food so the eaglets will learn to find food for themselves. The eaglets retain their dark coloring for several years, even as they grow larger. Only after they are five years old will they have the distinctive white, brown, and yellow markings of an adult bird. Bald eagles can live for up to forty years in the wild.

Down-covered eaglet

Immature bald eagle (left)
with mature bald eagle

17

Threatened by Extinction

An estimated 500,000 bald eagles populated North America when European settlers first arrived. As early as the mid-1600s, records show that bald eagles were being shot as pests and for food. The settlers believed the bald eagles were killing livestock, but bald eagles typically avoid human habitats and eat only carrion, fish, and small wildlife. As a matter of fact, bald eagles help ranchers and farmers by consuming field mice and other pests that damage crops and grain stores.

WANTED

50¢

For killing and eating livestock, chickens, game birds, and rabbits and other fur-bearing species. Death by shooting, poisoning, or trapping acceptable.

As human populations increased, *deforestation* made *nesting habitats* for bald eagles shrink. Dams, overfishing, and water pollution affected the food source – spawning fish – upon which bald eagles depended. Bald eagle populations began to decline. In 1940, the Bald Eagle Protection Act was passed to help protect the eagles' habitat and food sources. But by then, an entirely new danger had arisen, one that threatened to wipe out the bald eagle population in North America – *DDT*.

Water pollution

Fish killed by water pollution

Dams impact bald eagles'
food supply – spawning fish.

Deforestation destroys nesting habitats.

21

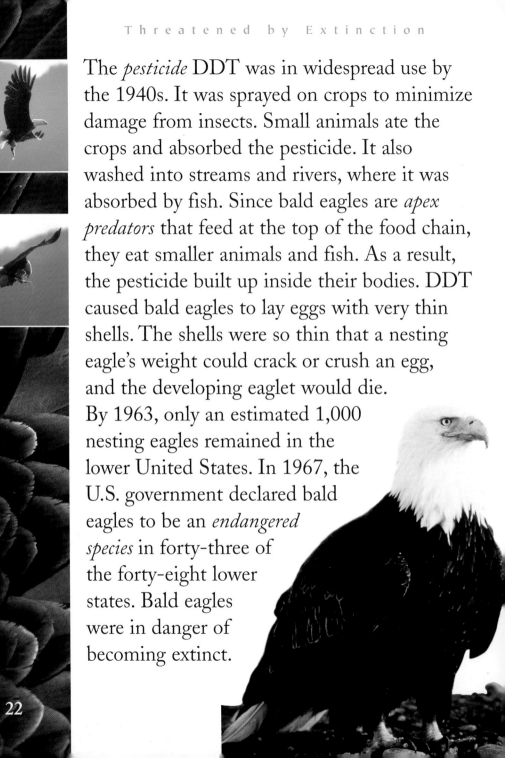

The *pesticide* DDT was in widespread use by the 1940s. It was sprayed on crops to minimize damage from insects. Small animals ate the crops and absorbed the pesticide. It also washed into streams and rivers, where it was absorbed by fish. Since bald eagles are *apex predators* that feed at the top of the food chain, they eat smaller animals and fish. As a result, the pesticide built up inside their bodies. DDT caused bald eagles to lay eggs with very thin shells. The shells were so thin that a nesting eagle's weight could crack or crush an egg, and the developing eaglet would die. By 1963, only an estimated 1,000 nesting eagles remained in the lower United States. In 1967, the U.S. government declared bald eagles to be an *endangered species* in forty-three of the forty-eight lower states. Bald eagles were in danger of becoming extinct.

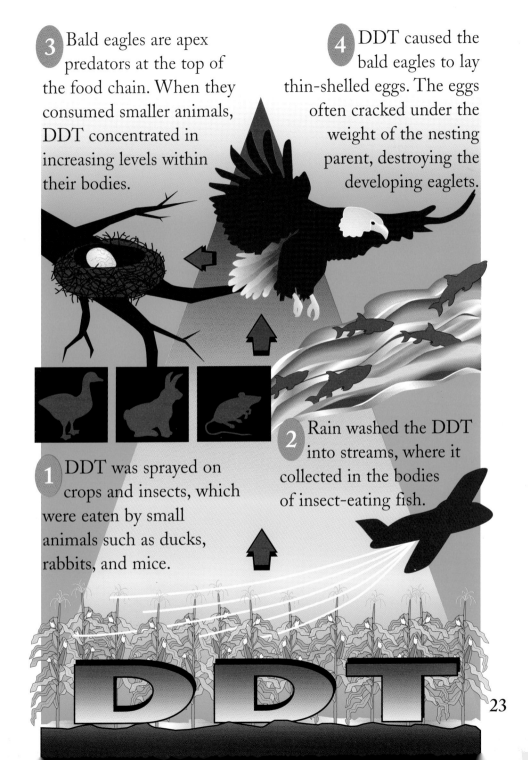

3 Bald eagles are apex predators at the top of the food chain. When they consumed smaller animals, DDT concentrated in increasing levels within their bodies.

4 DDT caused the bald eagles to lay thin-shelled eggs. The eggs often cracked under the weight of the nesting parent, destroying the developing eaglets.

1 DDT was sprayed on crops and insects, which were eaten by small animals such as ducks, rabbits, and mice.

2 Rain washed the DDT into streams, where it collected in the bodies of insect-eating fish.

DDT

Making a Comeback

By 1972, the use of DDT was banned in the United States and Canada. As the pesticide was slowly removed from the *environment*, bald eagle populations began to recover and increase. Still, many problems plagued the birds. Bald eagles continued to lose nesting habitat, and were still being hunted and trapped illegally. Many bald eagles suffered *lead poisoning* from eating animals that had been shot by hunters using lead pellets. Other chemicals and pesticides, such as oil and *PCBs*, hurt the bald eagle populations as well.

Chemical contamination

This bald eagle
was killed in an oil spill.

Dead bald eagles

25

Slowly, however, the bald eagles are making a comeback. Laws such as the Clean Water Act help to protect the bald eagles' habitat and food sources. Dams are modified to increase the presence of fish for the bald eagles to consume. In many places,

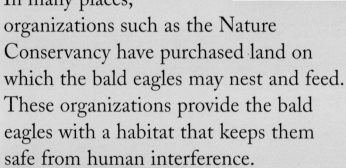

organizations such as the Nature Conservancy have purchased land on which the bald eagles may nest and feed. These organizations provide the bald eagles with a habitat that keeps them safe from human interference.

26

Reforestation project

27

Other organizations provide *reintroduction programs* that raise eaglets and then release them into the wild. Employing a process called *hacking*, people provide the eaglets with a protected nest and

These eaglets are being transferred to a reintroduction program

feed them until they are ready to fly away and fend for themselves. Programs such as these have helped the bald eagle halt its fall toward extinction. Today, more than 16,000 bald eagles live in the United States and Canada – more than ten times the number that existed only thirty years ago!

This eaglet is being fed by its handler.

This bald eagle is being released into the wild.

Immature eagle in protected nest

29

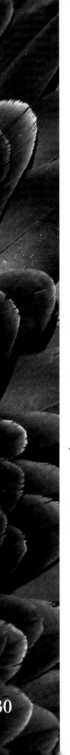

Glossary

- **aerie** – a large nest on a cliff or in a tall tree
- **apex predator** – a predator that exists at the top of a food chain
- **beak** – the rigid projecting mouth structure of birds and similar animals
- **brooding** – the act of sitting on and incubating eggs
- **carrion** – dead animal flesh, often eaten by scavengers
- **courtship display** – an elaborate display in which two eagles court by locking talons and cartwheeling through the air
- **DDT** – a pesticide that accumulated in the food chain and harmed raptor populations by causing thin-shelled eggs to be laid
- **deforestation** – the depletion of forest landscape and wildlife habitat through logging and similar activities
- **down** – small, extremely fluffy and soft feathers that cover young birds before they grow mature feathers
- **eaglet** – a young eagle that is still covered with down, confined to the nest, and dependent on its parents for food
- **endangered species** – an official label for species that are in danger of extinction
- **environment** – the complex biological factors that surround and affect an organism
- **extinction** – the complete and irreversible destruction of all living members of a given species

- **flyways** – the aerial pathways birds follow along their migratory routes
- **hacking** – the process of collecting, raising, and reintroducing raptors into the wild
- **lead poisoning** – an acute and sometimes fatal poisoning that occurs when lead is eaten
- **nesting habitat** – the necessary environmental surroundings and materials that support the building of an aerie and the feeding and raising of young
- **PCBs** – chemical compounds once used in paints, adhesives, and insulation that cause disease and birth defects in humans and animals
- **pesticide** – a chemical or organic compound used to kill pest insects and animals
- **prey** – an animal that is a source of food to another animal
- **raptor** – a bird of prey
- **reintroduction program** – a structured program in which wildlife is collected, raised in captivity, and released into the wild
- **spawn** – the act of producing, fertilizing, and depositing eggs by an aquatic animal
- **talon** – the claw of a bird of prey
- **territory** – the area surrounding a nest that is defended by a bird or other animal
- **wingspan** – the measure of a bird's body taken from wing tip to wing tip

About
Buck Wilde

My childhood home was Bald Eagle Valley, Pennsylvania. My grandmother told me stories of the magnificent raptors that soared over the valley long ago, but not once did I see a bald eagle when I was growing up. Now, nearly half a century later, bald eagles are once again flying over Bald Eagle Valley.

The night sky was filled with stars when I arrived on the Alaskan coast to photograph bald eagles attracted by a run of spawning salmon. At sunrise, I was ready to capture their magnificent image on film. It was a spectacular wilderness experience.

To me, bald eagles symbolize hope for other endangered species that exist on the brink of extinction. Their remarkable recovery proves that we can make a positive difference in the natural world if we all work together toward a common goal.

Written by **Buck Wilde**
Photographed by **Buck Wilde**
Edited by **David Nuss**
Designed by **Pat Madorin**

Additional photography by **American Numismatic Association:** (coins, p. 3); **Frank Oberle Photography:** (background feathers, cover, title page, borders; eagle talons, p. 9; courtship display, p. 13); **N.Z. Picture Library:** (bald eagle eggs, p. 14; p. 21); **Stock Photos:** (p. 2); **U.S. Fish and Wildlife Service:** (p. 12; p. 20; pp. 24-25; pp. 28-29); **Wolfgang Kaehler:** (reforestation, p. 27)

05 04 03 02 01 00 99
11 10 9 8 7 6 5 4 3 2

Distributed in the United States of America by
Rigby
a division of Reed Elsevier Inc.
P.O. Box 797
Crystal Lake, IL 60039-0797

Printed by Colorcraft, Hong Kong
ISBN: 1-57257-658-8